MW00387314

PRELUDES
FOR PIANO

7 Intermediate Pieces
that Explore and
Develop Lyrical Playing

Catherine Rollin

Preludes for Piano, Book Two, contains intermediate pieces that explore the use of patterns and the development of lyrical playing. They use many indications (*ritardando, accelerando, crescendo, diminuendo*, etc.) to assist in that development and to help the performer reflect upon the emotional character of each prelude. I hope that this collection will encourage many new discoveries in musical expression for students.

Alfred Music Publishing Co., Inc.
P.O. Box 10003
Van Nuys, CA 91410-0003
alfred.com

ISBN-10: 0-7390-8740-1
ISBN-13: 978-0-7390-8740-4

Prelude No. 1 in G Minor

Catherine Rollin

*Bring out top note in RH.

Prelude No. 2 in B-flat Major

Catherine Rollin

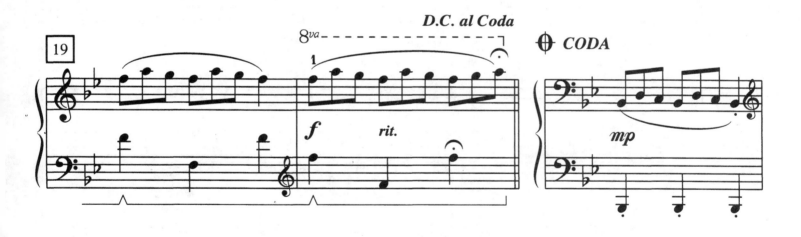

Prelude No. 3 in D Major

Catherine Rollin

*After D.C., the RH in measures 1 and 2 plays one octave higher on 1st repeat only, then as written.

Prelude No. 4 in A-flat Major

Catherine Rollin

Prelude No. 5 in E Minor

Catherine Rollin

Prelude No. 6 in F Minor

Catherine Rollin

Prelude No. 7 in A Major

Catherine Rollin

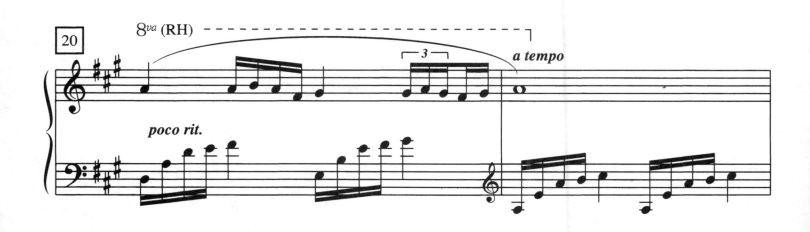

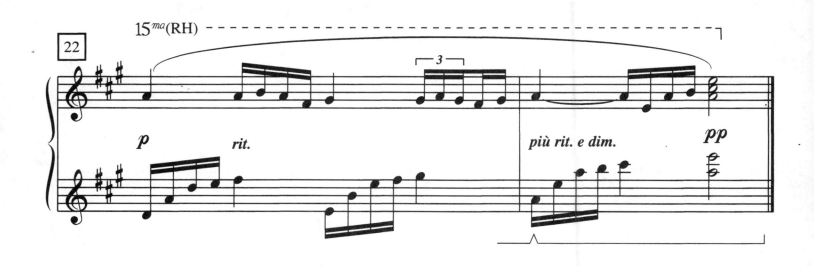